Cocoa Curios: Hope and Desire

Tanzania Ertel

BookLeaf Publishing

India | USA | UK

Presentation by *BookLeaf Publishing*

Web: www.bookleafpub.com

E-mail: info@bookleafpub.com

ISBN: 978-93-5744-971-7

First edition 2022

DEDICATION

To my forever Fox: may the den we've made stay warm from the heat of our hearts, stay grounded from my earth, and nourished by your water. Always.

ACKNOWLEDGEMENT

My mother and my father are the poets of my life.

PREFACE

Love notes, but brief
Keep poetic justice in linger

The Marshall

To willingly suffer with another is to embody that beings pain. It's still quite a strange occurrence to personify, in even the most light-filled of dawns. It is to evolve into that of which is rare morality. Calm, kind, enduring. It is the most tender act one can commit. It prevails as a tolerance among intimate mercy. And though this mercy navigates quietly, never crude or disruptive or demanding, the results of its compassion are vast and substantial. Cloth cut from the fairly traded goods of eternal gratitude.

And I am forever grateful.

When my spirit darkens in the dusk, when my heart cries out in anguish, when my body is undermined by trauma, My Marshall comes for me. Like a slated knight covered in honor and rampant on horseback, like a parched western hero ready to quick draw his pistol upon any threat, like a brooding warrior with royal blood and a heart of gold, like the greatest American captain worthy of celestial tools alongside his very own shield... He is there for me. He wishes for no noise or parade for his grace, but accepts all the stillness offered through gratitude.

And I am forever grateful.

As I suffer, he suffers. Yet somehow, he revolts. He fights for my wellness because in that moment, I need it. Stoic, capable, secure. Glorious in his calm authority, his kind words, and his otherworldly endurance. Vigorous in grace he is; so I call him "Your Grace". An heirloom of a man with a nature from another time, tending to my emotive necessities like a Marshall does his beloved city. The entirety of the human language does not permit nor license me the ability to describe my gratitude.

But I am forever grateful.

A Ray of Songshine

And all at once, my mind and my heart began to sing. Lowly, softly, with intent. Then louder, in chorus, with soul. The dutiful melody began flowing upward and outward from me, my signature vibration matching with that of The Source.

Miraculous light, radiating and beaming from my crown and chest as the cosmic ballad played in my veins. Amorous chords drench my senses as I sway side by side with the harmony that is him; to the music that is us.

Pillow Peace

There is a sweetness in slumber, so slumber deep
my sweet

Serenity rests upon your countenance while the
the wind in your chest governs a gentle sway

The rise and fall of your silhouette evokes the
desire to outline the flesh on your bones

You stir, breathing. She purrs, needing.

Your body radiates a humble warmth that gives
rise to her most profound yearn and craving.

The curious miracle that is your truth helps to
hold her sap at it's basin.

You turn, yawning. She yawns, stirring.

Rest now together, in sync with the moments
cadence.

For there is a sweetness in slumber, so slumber
deep my sweet.

His Perspective

When I looked at her, I thought about myself and my lack of status. I watched in full awareness that I wasn't exactly impressive or stately like the man I had seen court her before.

"Successful", "debonair"... Those were words I had heard her use when asked what were attractive qualities in a man. I hoped my heart would be enough. I should walk away

She was so ample; her silhouette even hypnotizing in the sunlight. And such a hungry creature for knowledge yet completely earnest about life and learning from others.

She had everything I could ever ask for and she asked for nothing. Which only heightened her royal essence in my mind. She was a goddess of so many things, including physical beauty.

So Tell Her

I knew I stimulated her somehow. I made her interested in me beyond looks and money. I do believe my beloved grew tiresome of the world she was born into. A world of façades and champagne, of ruthless men, and unscrupulous women. A world not of peace and far from pure.

Despite looking like a perfect piece of the puzzle, I could tell she longed for a tradition and it's transformation to work honestly and reach authentic pleasure and live to speak of it, or maybe even change.

If it's Up

Let us count up from here my dear.

You may always ask much of me. I will allow it.

For to hear your voice say my name is restitution
through and through.

Beloved

I have longed for you most of my life.
To possess you would make my very existence
worthwhile.

Teach me, touch me, create life with me.

The salt of your skin paints my lips as I quiver
underneath you. I could swallow this moment let
it nourish all of me.

Feed me, feel me, put life back inside me.

Clarity is never fully present in love's company.
May I tickle your back to see your flash rise in
beads. We need neither to be so clear nor any
company other than our own, measured only by
the weight of our rapture.

Tell me lover, tell me I'm the one, that I'm
unforgettable, and I will forever be yours.

Lift me love me, live or with me!

Bees and Flowers

It was as if I were a Yellow Jacket to a Calla Lily.

Buzzing all about her, attracted by her scent and the colorful stillness of her body.

Hungry for what was inside of her.

Battered Love

The moon was yellow as we rode on, back to the wrong way.

My tune was mellow as the doubt of the benefit seem to hit harms way.

And again I asked you for it

Oh again I asked you for it

Yes, again I begged you for your battered love.

Well at least it's some kind, some form of care.

It beats being beaten upon my high chair.

I am just tired of being clothed but feeling bare,

Bare in your battered love.

Mirror Tears

The girl with the biggest heart is the girl in the most pain

Her eyes well up with regret, her body twists in shame.

Her eyes once vibrant in light now only reflect the dark

The ugliness of failure has surely left its mark.

"I am not so fair", she screams but barely a whisper heard

"You swore in faith upon ardor, you gave me your word."

When love is not enough which it rarely seems to be

Trials of the pure falter, and then settles misery.

Her kindness taken for granted; her good deeds ridiculed

"Fool me twice shame on you", she says, "for I've been doubly fooled."

So take heed heartfelt femme whose spirits are being drained

For the girl with the biggest heart is the girl in the most pain.

Alanis

The sickened rage I felt for him was far more acidic than the most sour poison locked within any creature.

I hated him from the inside out. I loathed the very air he breathed, wishing I could stifle the science of oxygen entirely, but only in his vicinity.

Nature's Way

Opal and chocolate fused at once, creating an intimate honesty in the moment their eyes met.

She was breathing unsteadily, feeling staggered in appearance and embarrassed to not know what she looked like as she passed by his perfect, sweet face.

And...Oh, what a face. Dark, yet gentle. Like a stormy twilight sky, he was a man of earth's dust: Black and beautiful

Eyes cut like diamonds, this sweet-faced man held a grip upon her.

Inside she winced, feeling so much in only seconds, but in capable of expressing any of it.

Left, It's Right

My dress was off when you boldly told me you could not help me.

But this messy love is the one thing only I have to lift me.

Not Like the Flower

Forget me not, because I'm right next to you.

My heart just stopped, is this all a test to you?

And if it's not, then change the way I am hurting.

I'll give you the best of me

And all I want is for you to stop questioning

Whether or not you love me in the same way

Oh, forget me not

Chocolate for breakfast

Shimmer shine goes my cocoa flesh

As beads of wet passion gather

You could have been anywhere in the world but you're here with me

It must be my sable skin that you're after

Your answer swarms upon me in the form of a soft bite

Dessert for our first meal is quite rich in flavor

Bamboo and fresh fruit is added to our swirl and delight

Love Note in Brief

Though mountains are high

My beating heart flies higher

Elevated from all the noise.

Me and the clouds conspire

Pronewa

Prosperity needs warmth in the same regardthat
rain requires the thick padding of the earth to fall
upon and bounce off of. This is balance.

La Vida

What is the meaning of life? More simply stated than one may think. The meaning of life is to commit to living out whatever unique yet collective experience that unfolds throughout your days. That's it. The commitment to living.

Let Me Slip Away

{{Poem 19}} When left to her own devices, a major shift in energy rings about, vibrating her head and heart. Please, don't let her go. Don't forget her in the moments when the moon is full and water meets the edge of the earth.

www.ingramcontent.com/pod-product-compliance
Lightning Source LLC
LaVergne TN
LVHW021347200726
843509LV00014B/2719